S

Si

Spanish

1

Similar
Spanish-English
Words

Des Meagher
Beverley Roberts

C000200920

Super Simple Spanish ™

This edition first published in 2014.

ISBN 13 978-0-9552198-7-0

Printed and bound in Spain.

For more information about the
Super Simple Spanish series of books
please see our website:

www.supersimplespanish.com

Contents

Introduction

The Super Simple Spanish series of books is designed to make Spanish as simple as possible.

Super Simple Spanish No 1 Similar Words has:

Spanish Vocabulary

Over 1200 useful identical and similar Spanish-English words.

Spanish Pronunciation

Simple Spanish pronunciation and how word stress is used.

Spain Guide

The highlights of Spain with maps of mainland Spain and the Spanish Islands.

The Authors

We love Spain. We try and visit as often as we can. We've worked in Madrid and Seville and spent a small fortune on books over the years trying to improve our Spanish.

Some Spanish books are good and some are not so good. What all our Spanish books have in common is that they are in a drawer somewhere and we never use them. How does that happen?

We took another look at our Spanish books and the answer became clear. Very few of our Spanish books are simple and none of them are super simple. So, starting with vocabulary, we decided to produce a series of books that really would make Spanish Super Simple.

Super Simple Spanish

Each book in the Super Simple Spanish series gives you simple **Spanish Vocabulary**, simple **Spanish Pronunciation** and our **Spain Guide** highlighting the very best of Spain.

The first 3 books in this series are:

No 1. Similar Words
Over 1200 useful words that are amazingly similar in Spanish and English.

No 2. Essential Words
Over 1200 basic and essential Spanish words grouped together under 75 simple headings.

No 3. Important Words
Over 1200 important Spanish words carefully chosen to expand your Spanish vocabulary.

SPANISH VOCABULARY

Spanish-English Identical and Similar Words
A-Z

PLEASE NOTE

The Spanish Words section has many Spanish words that end in o. Words ending in o are usually masculine in Spanish.

There are also many words that end in a in Spanish and these words are usually feminine.

Some Spanish words can end in o or a if they are used in the masculine and the feminine.

For example,

amigo = male friend
amiga = female friend

camarero = waiter
camarera = waitress

To keep the Spanish Vocabulary section as simple as possible we have used the masculine ending o for words that can be used in the masculine and the feminine.

ACCESS ▶

access	acceso
accident	accidente
actor	actor
actress	actriz
additive	aditivo
adhesive	adhesivo
adjective	adjetivo
adult	adulto
adventure	aventura
adverb	adverbio
Africa	África
African	africano

agency	agencia
agent	agente
air	aire
air–conditioning	aire acondicionado
airport	aeropuerto
alarm	alarma
album	álbum
alcohol	alcohol
alert	alerta
allergic	alérgico
allergy	alergia

almond	almendra
alphabet	alfabeto
ambulance	ambulancia
anchovy	anchoa
angle	ángulo
animal	animal
anniversary	aniversario
annual	anual
anorak	anorak
antenna	antena
antibiotic	antibiótico
antiseptic	antiséptico

APARTMENT ▸

apartment	apartamento
April	abril
architect	arquitecto
art	arte
artist	artista
arthritis	artritis
artificial	artificial
asparagus	espárrago
aspirin	aspirina
association	asociación
asthma	asma
Athens	Atenas

athlete	atleta
atlas	atlas
attractive	atractivo
August	agosto
Australia	Australia
Australian	australiano
authentic	auténtico
author	autor
autobiography	autobiografía
automatic	automático
autumn	otoño
avenue	avenida

A VERBS

to accept	aceptar
to activate	activar
to adapt	adaptar
to adjust	ajustar
to admire	admirar
to affect	afectar
to approve	aprobar
to authorize	autorizar

BABY ▶

baby	bebé
bacon	bacon
balcony	balcón
Balearic Islands	Islas Baleares
ball	balón
bamboo	bambú
band	banda
bank	banco
bar	bar
barbecue	barbacoa
barrel	barril

barrier	barrera
base	base
baseball	béisbol
basic	básico
bat	bate
battery(car)	batería
battle	batalla
bay	bahía
beard	barba
Belgian	belga
Belgium	Bélgica
Belgrade	Belgrado

bestseller	bestseller
bicycle	bicicleta
bike	bici
bidet	bidet
bifocals	bifocales
bikini	bikini
bilingual	bilingüe
bingo	bingo
binoculars	binoculares
biography	biografía
biology	biología
block	bloque

BLOUSE ▸

blouse	blusa
bomb	bomba
boot	bota
bottle	botella
boulevard	bulevar
bowl	bol
boxing	boxeo
boycott	boicot
brandy	brandy
Brazil	Brasil
Brazilian	brasileño
breeze	brisa

brilliant	brillante
Britain	Gran Bretaña
British	británico
broadband	banda ancha
broccoli	brócoli
bronze	bronce
brooch	broche
Brussels	Bruselas
buffet	buffet
bus	autobús
butane	butano
button	botón

B VERBS

to baptize	bautizar
to base	basar
to beat	batir
to benefit	beneficiar
to block	bloquear
to bottle	embotellar
to box	boxear
to boycott	boicotear

CABLE ▸

cable	cable
calcium	calcio
calculator	calculadora
calendar	calendario
camper	campista
campsite	camping
Canary Islands	Islas Canarias
cancelled	cancelado
cannelloni	canelones
cape	cabo
capital	capital

cappuccino	capuchino
captain	capitán
carnival	carnaval
carpenter	carpintero
castle	castillo
cathedral	catedral
cauliflower	coliflor
cave	cueva
centenary	centenario
centigrade	centígrado
centilitre	centilitro
centimetre	centímetro

central	céntrico
centre	centro
ceramics	cerámica
cereals	cereales
champion	campeón
charger	cargador
charity	caridad
cheque	cheque
chimney	chimenea
China	China
Chinese	chino
chocolate	chocolate

cider	sidra
cigarette	cigarrillo
cinema	cine
circle	círculo
circular	circular
circus	circo
client	cliente
climate	clima
clinic	clínica
club	club
coast	costa
cocktail	cóctel

COCONUT ▸

coconut	coco
coffee	café
colleague	colega
colour	color
committee	comité
community	comunidad
concert	concierto
confidential	confidencial
confirmation	confirmación
connection	conexión
consecutive	consecutivo
consulate	consulado

CONTENTS ▸

contents	contenido
continent	continente
contract	contrato
copy	copia
correct	correcto
cost	coste
course	curso
croissant	croissant
culture	cultura
curry	curry
curtain	cortina
curve	curva

C VERBS

to cancel	cancelar
to confirm	confirmar
to connect	conectar
to continue	continuar
to copy	copiar
to cost	costar
to cross	cruzar
to cut	cortar

Danish	danés
data	datos
database	base de datos
day	día
debit	débito
debut	debut
decade	década
decaffeinated	descafeinado
December	diciembre
defect	defecto
delicate	delicado
delicious	delicioso

DENMARK ▶

Denmark	Dinamarca
dentist	dentista
deodorant	desodorante
department	departamento
design	diseño
destination	destino
detail	detalle
detergent	detergente
diabetes	diabetes
diabetic	diabético
diagonal	diagonal
diagram	diagrama

diameter	diámetro
diarrhoea	diarrea
dictionary	diccionario
diesel	diesel
diet	dieta
different	diferente
difficult	difícil
digital	digital
dimension	dimensión
direct	directo
disconnection	desconexión
discount	descuento

DISINFECTANT ▶

disinfectant	desinfectante
dispute	disputa
distance	distancia
divorce	divorcio
document	documento
dollar	dólar
dose	dosis
double	doble
doughnut	donut
dozen	docena
duplicate	duplicado
during	durante

D VERBS

to decide	decidir
to depend	depender
to describe	describir
to disconnect	desconectar
to discover	descubrir
to disinfect	desinfectar
to divide	dividir
to donate	donar

east	este
edition	edición
effect	efecto
effective	eficaz
efficient	eficiente
electrician	electricista
electricity	electricidad
elegant	elegante
elephant	elefante
email	email
embassy	embajada
emergency	emergencia

employee	empleado
employer	empleador
employment	empleo
energy	energía
engineer	ingeniero
England	Inglaterra
English	inglés
enormous	enorme
entrance	entrada
equal	igual
equator	ecuador
equivalent	equivalente

error	error
euro	euro
Europe	Europa
European	europeo
exact	exacto
exactly	exactamente
exam	examen
example	ejemplo
excellent	excelente
except	excepto
excess	exceso
excessive	excesivo

EXCLUSIVE ▸

exclusive	exclusivo
excursion	excursión
excuse	excusa
exhibition	exposición
exotic	exótico
expatriate	expatriado
experience	experiencia
expert	experto
explanation	explicación
express	expreso
expression	expresión
extreme	extremo

E VERBS

to educate	educar
to email	emailear
to employ	emplear
to enter	entrar
to escape	escapar
to exist	existir
to explain	explicar
to extend	extender

fabulous	fabuloso
false	falso
fame	fama
family	familia
famous	famoso
fantastic	fantástico
fascinating	fascinante
fatigue	fatiga
favour	favor
favourite	favorito
fax	fax
February	febrero

federation	federación
ferry	ferry
festival	festival
fever	fiebre
fibre	fibra
fiction	ficción
fillet	filete
final	final
finalist	finalista
finance	finanzas
Finland	Finlandia
Finnish	finlandés

FIXED ▶

fixed	fijo
flexible	flexible
florist's	floristería
flower	flor
fluoride	fluoruro
football	fútbol
footballer	futbolista
formal	formal
format	formato
foundation	fundación
fountain	fuente
fracture	fractura

fragile	frágil
fragrance	fragancia
France	Francia
fraud	fraude
French	francés
frequent	frecuente
fresh	fresco
fried	frito
frontier	frontera
fruit	fruta
fundamental	fundamental
future	futuro

F VERBS

to fax	faxear
to film	filmar
to filter	filtrar
to finance	financiar
to float	flotar
to format	formatear
to fracture	fracturar
to fry	freír

GALLERY ▸

gallery	galería
garage	garaje
garden	jardín
gardener	jardinero
gas	gas
gel	gel
general	general
generation	generación
generator	generador
generous	generoso
Geneva	Ginebra
genius	genio

geography	geografía
geology	geología
geometry	geometría
geranium	geranio
gesture	gesto
giant	gigante
gigantic	gigantesco
gin	ginebra
gin and tonic	gin-tonic
ginger ale	ginger ale
ginseng	ginseng
global	global

glucose	glucosa
gluten	gluten
goal	gol
golf	golf
golfer	golfista
golf club	club de golf
government	gobierno
governor	gobernador
gradual	gradual
gram	gramo
grammar	gramática
granite	granito

GRAPH ▶

graph	gráfico
grey	gris
grease	grasa
Greece	Grecia
Greek	griego
group	grupo
guarantee	garantía
guaranteed	garantizado
guide	guía
guitar	guitarra
gulf	golfo
gym	gimnasio

G VERBS

to gallop	galopar
to generalize	generalizar
to generate	generar
to gesticulate	gesticular
to govern	gobernar
to grease	engrasar
to guarantee	garantizar
to guide	guiar

habitat	hábitat
hacker	hacker
halogen	halógeno
hamburger	hamburguesa
hamster	hámster
harness	arnés
hectare	hectárea
helicopter	helicóptero
hello	hola
hemisphere	hemisferio
herb	hierba
herbalist's	herbolario

hero	héroe
heroic	heroico
hexagon	hexágono
hexagonal	hexagonal
historic	histórico
history	historia
hobby	hobby
hockey	hockey
Holland	Holanda
hologram	holograma
honour	honor
honourable	honorable

horizon	horizonte
horizontal	horizontal
hormone	hormona
horoscope	horóscopo
horrendous	horrendo
horrible	horrible
hospital	hospital
hospitality	hospitalidad
hostile	hostil
hotel	hotel
hour	hora
human	humano

humanity	humanidad
humble	humilde
humid	húmedo
humidity	humedad
hurricane	huracán
hybrid	híbrido
hydrogen	hidrógeno
hygiene	higiene
hygienic	higiénico
hypermarket	hipermercado
hypnosis	hipnosis
hypocrite	hipócrita

H VERBS

to hallucinate	alucinar
to harmonize	armonizar
to hibernate	hibernar
to honour	honrar
to horrify	horrorizar
to hospitalize	hospitalizar
to humiliate	humillar
to hypnotize	hipnotizar

IDEA ▸

idea	idea
ideal	ideal
identical	idéntico
identification	identificación
identity	identidad
illegal	ilegal
image	imagen
imagination	imaginación
immediate	inmediato
important	importante
impossible	imposible
impressive	impresionante

INCIDENT ▸

incident	incidente
included	incluido
incorrect	incorrecto
incredible	increíble
independent	independiente
index	índice
indigestion	indigestión
infection	infección
inflammable	inflamable
inflammation	inflamación
inflation	inflación
ingredient	ingrediente

inhaler	inhalador
initial	inicial
injection	inyección
innocent	inocente
insect	insecto
insomnia	insomnio
instinct	instinto
institute	instituto
insulin	insulina
insult	insulto
intelligent	inteligente
intense	intenso

interest	interés
interesting	interesante
international	internacional
interpreter	intérprete
inventory	inventario
invitation	invitación
Ireland	Irlanda
Irish	irlandés
island	isla
Italian	italiano
Italy	Italia
itinerary	itinerario

I VERBS

to include	incluir
to inform	informar
to insist	insistir
to inspect	inspeccionar
to install	instalar
to insult	insultar
to invite	invitar
to irritate	irritar

JACKET ▶

jacket	chaqueta
jacuzzi	jacuzzi
Japan	Japón
Japanese	japonés
jasmine	jazmín
jazz	jazz
jockey	jockey
judo	judo
July	julio
June	junio
jungle	jungla
justice	justicia

karaoke	karaoke
karate	karate
ketchup	ketchup
kilo	kilo
kilobyte	kilobyte
kilogram	kilogramo
kilometre	kilómetro
kilowatt	kilovatio
kiosk	kiosco
kiwi fruit	kiwi
Korea	Corea
Korean	coreano

lamp	lámpara
lasagne	lasaña
laser	láser
latitude	latitud
launderette	lavandería
laxative	laxante
leader	líder
league	liga
legal	legal
legend	leyenda
lemon	limón
lentils	lentejas

lesson	lección
lettuce	lechuga
liberty	libertad
licence	licencia
ligament	ligamento
lilac	lila
lime	lima
limit	límite
line	línea
lingerie	lencería
lion	león
liqueur	licor

liquid	líquido
Lisbon	Lisboa
list	lista
litre	litro
logical	lógico
logistics	logística
logo	logotipo
London	Londres
longitude	longitud
lotion	loción
lottery	lotería
lycra	lycra

L VERBS

to legalize	legalizar
to legislate	legislar
to legitimize	legitimar
to liberalize	liberalizar
to liberate	liberar
to limit	limitar
to locate	localizar
to lubricate	lubricar

macaroni	macarrones
machine	máquina
magnificent	magnífico
mango	mango
map	mapa
marathon	maratón
marble	mármol
March	marzo
margarine	margarina
market	mercado
marvellous	maravillosa
marzipan	mazapán

maximum	máximo
May	mayo
mayonnaise	mayonesa
mechanic	mecánico
Mediterranean	mediterráneo
melon	melón
menthol	mentol
message	mensaje
metre	metro
midday	mediodía
midnight	medianoche
migraine	migraña

mile	milla
milligram	miligramo
millilitre	mililitro
millimetre	milímetro
million	millón
minestrone	minestrone
minibus	microbús
minimum	mínimo
mint	menta
minute	minuto
mobile phone	móvil
modern	moderno

moment	momento
monument	monumento
Moscow	Moscú
mosquito	mosquito
mountain	montaña
mountainous	montañoso
much	mucho
municipal	municipal
muscle	músculo
museum	museo
music	música
mustard	mostaza

M VERBS

to maintain	mantener
to maximize	maximizar
to memorize	memorizar
to minimize	minimizar
to modernize	modernizar
to modify	modificar
to motivate	motivar
to multiply	multiplicar

name	nombre
nation	nación
national	nacional
nationality	nacionalidad
natural	natural
nature	naturaleza
nausea	náusea
necessary	necesario
necessity	necesidad
nectar	néctar
nectarine	nectarina
negative	negativo

NEGLIGENCE ▸

negligence	negligencia
negotiable	negociable
negotiation	negociación
nerve	nervio
nervous	nervioso
New York	Nueva York
New Zealand	Nueva Zelanda
niche	nicho
nickel	níquel
nicotine	nicotina
nitrogen	nitrógeno
no	no

NORMAL ▶

normal	normal
normality	normalidad
normally	normalmente
north	norte
northeast	noreste
northwest	noroeste
Norway	Noruega
Norwegian	noruego
nostalgia	nostalgia
nostalgic	nostálgico
notary	notario
note	nota

notification	notificación
notion	noción
notional	nocional
novel	novela
novelist	novelista
November	noviembre
nuclear	nuclear
number	número
numerous	numeroso
nutrition	nutrición
nutritious	nutritivo
nylon	nylon

N VERBS

to narrate	narrar
to nationalize	nacionalizar
to naturalize	naturalizar
to navigate	navegar
to negotiate	negociar
to notice	notar
to notify	notificar
to number	numerar

OBJECT ▶

object	objeto
objection	objeción
obligation	obligación
obscure	oscuro
observation	observación
observer	observador
obsession	obsesión
obsolete	obsoleto
obstacle	obstáculo
obstruction	obstrucción
obvious	obvio
obviously	obviamente

occasion	ocasión
occupation	ocupación
ocean	océano
octagon	octágono
octagonal	octagonal
October	octubre
offensive	ofensivo
offer	oferta
office	oficina
official	oficial
officially	oficialmente
on line	en línea

operator	operador
opinion	opinión
opportunist	oportunista
opportunity	oportunidad
opposition	oposición
oppressive	opresivo
optician's	óptica
optimism	optimismo
optimist	optimista
optimum	óptimo
option	opción
optional	opcional

oregano	orégano
organic	orgánico
organization	organización
organized	organizado
origin	origen
original	original
originally	originalmente
osteopath	osteópata
ounce	onza
oxygen	oxígeno
oyster	ostra
ozone	ozono

O VERBS

to observe	observar
to obstruct	obstruir
to obtain	obtener
to occupy	ocupar
to offend	ofender
to offer	ofrecer
to omit	omitir
to organize	organizar

package	paquete
page	página
painter	pintor
pair	par
palace	palacio
pale	pálido
panic	pánico
paper	papel
paracetamol	paracetamol
paradise	paraíso
parallel	paralelo
park	parque

parking	aparcamiento
parliament	parlamento
passenger	pasajero
passion	pasión
passport	pasaporte
pathetic	patético
patience	paciencia
patient	paciente
pause	pausa
pear	pera
penicillin	penicilina
pensioner	pensionista

per cent	por ciento
percentage	porcentaje
perfect	perfecto
perfume	perfume
permanent	permanente
person	persona
personal	personal
pessimist	pesimista
pharmacy	farmacia
phase	fase
photo	foto
photocopy	fotocopia

phrase	frase
picnic	picnic
piece	pieza
pilot	piloto
pine	pino
pineapple	piña
pint	pinta
plan	plan
planet	planeta
plant	planta
plastic	plástico
plate	plato

point	punto
Poland	Polonia
Polish	polaco
police	policía
pollen	polen
popular	popular
population	población
port	puerto
Portugal	Portugal
Portuguese	portugués
position	posición
positive	positivo

possible	posible
possibility	posibilidad
postcode	código postal
potato	patata
power	poder
president	presidente
pressure	presión
price	precio
prince	príncipe
princess	princesa
priority	prioridad
private	privado

probable	probable
probably	probablemente
problem	problema
programme	programa
promise	promesa
pronunciation	pronunciación
protection	protección
province	provincia
public	público
puncture	pinchazo
pure	puro
pyjamas	pijama

P VERBS

to paint	pintar
to park	aparcar
to pay	pagar
to photocopy	fotocopiar
to practise	practicar
to prefer	preferir
to prepare	preparar
to pronounce	pronunciar

qualified	cualificado
quality	calidad
quantity	cantidad
quarantine	cuarentena
quarter	cuarto
quartet	cuarteto
quartz	cuarzo
questionnaire	cuestionario
quiche	quiche
quintet	quinteto
quorum	quórum
quota	cuota

RACKET ▸

racket	raqueta
radiator	radiador
radio	radio
ramp	rampa
ravioli	ravioles
realist	realista
reality	realidad
reason	razón
reasonable	razonable
receipt	recibo
recent	reciente
recently	recientemente

RECEPTION ▸

reception	recepción
receptionist	recepcionista
rechargeable	recargable
recipe	receta
recycling	reciclaje
refreshing	refrescante
region	región
regional	regional
relaxing	relajante
remote	remoto
renewable	renovable
republic	república

RESCUE ▸

rescue	rescate
reservation	reserva
resident	residente
respect	respeto
restaurant	restaurante
result	resultado
reversible	reversible
rhubarb	ruibarbo
rhyme	rima
rhythm	ritmo
rich	rico
ridiculous	ridículo

rigid	rígido
risk	riesgo
risotto	risotto
rival	rival
river	río
robbery	robo
rock	roca
rocky	rocoso
Romania	Rumania
Romanian	rumano
Rome	Roma
rose	rosa

ROSÉ WINE ▶

rosé wine	vino rosado
round	redondo
route	ruta
routine	rutina
royal	real
rugby	rugby
ruin	ruina
rumour	rumor
rural	rural
Russia	Rusia
Russian	ruso
rustic	rústico

R VERBS

to receive	recibir
to recharge	recargar
to recommend	recomendar
to recycle	reciclar
to reduce	reducir
to repeat	repetir
to reserve	reservar
to rob	robar

SACCHARIN ▶

saccharin	sacarina
salad	ensalada
salmon	salmón
salt	sal
salted	salado
sandal	sandalia
sardine	sardina
satellite	satélite
satin	satén
Saturday	sábado
sauce	salsa
second	segundo

secret	secreto
section	sección
security	seguridad
sedative	sedante
semifinal	semifinal
Senate	Senado
senator	senador
sensational	sensacional
sensor	sensor
September	septiembre
series	serie
serious	serio

service	servicio
serviette	servilleta
seventy	setenta
shampoo	champú
silence	silencio
similar	similar
simple	simple
sincere	sincero
society	sociedad
soda water	soda
sodium	sodio
sofa	sofá

software	software
solar	solar
soldier	soldado
solid	sólido
soluble	soluble
sorbet	sorbete
soup	sopa
south	sur
South Africa	Suráfrica
South America	Suramérica
southeast	sudeste
southwest	sudoeste

soya	soja
spaghetti	espaguetis
Spain	España
Spanish	español
special	especial
spice	especia
spinach	espinaca
splendid	espléndido
sport	deporte
stadium	estadio
station	estación
sterile	estéril

stomach	estómago
stress	estrés
student	estudiante
style	estilo
sugar	azúcar
super	super
supermarket	supermercado
supplement	suplemento
surprise	sorpresa
symptom	síntoma
synthetic	sintético
system	sistema

S VERBS

to separate	separar
to serve	servir
to simplify	simplificar
to ski	esquiar
to sterilize	esterilizar
to study	estudiar
to suffer	sufrir
to suggest	sugerir

tattoo	tatuaje
taxi	taxi
tea	té
telephone	teléfono
television	televisión
temperature	temperatura
temptation	tentación
tendon	tendón
tennis	tenis
tense	tenso
tension	tensión
tequila	tequila

terminal	terminal
terrace	terraza
textile	textil
texture	textura
theatre	teatro
therapy	terapia
thermometer	termómetro
thermostat	termostato
tiger	tigre
toast	tostada
toaster	tostadora
tobacco	tabaco

tomato	tomate
total	total
tourism	turismo
tourist	turista
tournament	torneo
towel	toalla
tower	torre
tradition	tradición
traditional	tradicional
traffic	tráfico
train	tren
transfer	transferencia

treatment	tratamiento
trophy	trofeo
tropical	tropical
trout	trucha
tube	tubo
tulip	tulipán
tuna	atún
tunnel	túnel
Turkey	Turquía
Turkish	turco
type	tipo
typical	típico

T VERBS

to tattoo	tatuar
to televise	televisar
to toast	tostar
to tolerate	tolerar
to touch	tocar
to transfer	transferir
to transport	transportar
to trot	trotar

ULCER ▸

ulcer	úlcera
ultimatum	ultimátum
ultrasound	ultrasonido
ultraviolet	ultravioleta
unacceptable	inaceptable
unanimous	unánime
uncomfortable	incómodo
unconfirmed	no confirmado
unconscious	inconsciente
undulating	ondulante
unequal	desigual
unfortunate	desafortunado

unhygienic	antihigiénico
uniform	uniforme
uninterrupted	ininterrumpido
unique	único
unisex	unisex
unit	unidad
united	unido
United Kingdom	Reino Unido
United States	Estados Unidos
universal	universal
universe	universo
university	universidad

UNJUST ▶

unjust	injusto
unlimited	ilimitado
unnecessary	innecesario
unoccupied	desocupado
unofficial	no oficial
unpopular	impopular
unreal	irreal
unsafe	inseguro
unsatisfactory	insatisfactorio
unsociable	insociable
unsporting	antideportivo
unstable	inestable

unsure	inseguro
uranium	uranio
urban	urbano
urbanization	urbanización
urgency	urgencia
urgent	urgente
urgently	urgentemente
use	uso
used	usado
user	usuario
usual	usual
utensil	utensilio

U VERBS

to undulate	ondular
to unify	unificar
to unite	unir
to urbanize	urbanizar
to urge	urgir
to urinate	orinar
to use	usar
to utilize	utilizar

VACCINE ▸

vaccine	vacuna
valid	válido
valley	valle
valuable	valioso
value	valor
vanilla	vainilla
variety	variedad
varnish	barniz
vaseline	vaselina
vast	vasto
vegan	vegano
vegetarian	vegetariano

vehicle	vehículo
vein	vena
verb	verbo
verdict	veredicto
vermouth	vermut
versatile	versátil
version	versión
vertical	vertical
vertigo	vértigo
vet	veterinario
veteran	veterano
veto	veto

VIA ▶

via	vía
viaduct	viaducto
victim	víctima
victory	victoria
vinaigrette	vinagreta
vinegar	vinagre
violence	violencia
virus	virus
visa	visado
visit	visita
visitor	visitante
vitamin	vitamina

VOCABULARY ▸

vocabulary	vocabulario
vodka	vodka
volcano	volcán
volley	volea
volleyball	vóleibol
volt	voltio
voltage	voltaje
volume	volumen
volunteer	voluntario
vote	voto
voter	votante
vowel	vocal

V VERBS

to vaccinate	vacunar
to value	valorar
to varnish	barnizar
to veto	vetar
to vibrate	vibrar
to visit	visitar
to vomit	vomitar
to vote	votar

WATT ▶

watt	vatio
wattage	vataje
webcam	webcam
west	oeste
whisky	whisky
X-rays	rayos X
yacht	yate
yoga	yoga
yogurt	yogur
zero	cero
zone	zona
zoo	zoo

Spanish Pronunciation

Pronunciation

Pronunciation Summary

Spanish Word Stress

Spanish Pronunciation

▪ ce

In Spanish ce is pronounced like the th in thanks.

Practise saying this th sound with these Spanish words:

cerca	near
cero	zero
cerdo	pig
centro	centre
cesta	basket

Spanish Pronunciation

▪ ci

In Spanish ci is pronounced
like the th in thanks.

Practise saying this th sound
with these Spanish words.

cinco	five
cita	appointment
cien	one hundred
circo	circus
circular	circular

Spanish Pronunciation

▪ e

In Spanish e at the end of a word is pronounced like a – the first letter of the English alphabet.

Practise saying this a sound with these Spanish words.

madre	mother
padre	father
coche	car
leche	milk
grande	big

Spanish Pronunciation

■ ge

In Spanish ge is pronounced like the ch in the Scottish word loch. This is a back-of-the-throat sound as if clearing the throat!

Practise saying this throaty loch sound with these Spanish words.

general	general
generoso	generous
genial	brilliant
gente	people
gel	gel

Spanish Pronunciation

gi

In Spanish gi is pronounced like the ch in the Scottish word loch. This is a back-of-the-throat sound as if clearing the throat!

Practise saying this throaty loch sound with these Spanish words.

ginebra	gin
gimnasta	gymnast
gimnasio	gym
gitano	gypsy
gira	tour

Spanish Pronunciation

▪ h

In Spanish h has no sound.
It is a silent letter.

Practise saying these Spanish
words making sure h has no
sound.

hola	hello
hora	hour
hoy	today
hombre	man
hospital	hospital

Spanish Pronunciation

▪ j

In Spanish j is pronounced like
the ch in the Scottish word loch.
This is a back-of-the throat sound
as if clearing the throat!

Practise saying this throaty loch
sound with these Spanish words.

jamón	ham
jardín	garden
jarra	jug
junio	June
julio	July

Spanish Pronunciation

▪ ll

In Spanish ll is pronounced like the y in yes.

Practise saying this y sound with these Spanish words.

tortilla	omelette
castillo	castle
cuchillo	knife
botella	bottle
caballo	horse

Spanish Pronunciation

. ñ

In Spanish ñ is pronounced like ny in canyon.

Practise saying this ny sound with these Spanish words.

España	Spain
mañana	tomorrow
montaña	mountain
piña	pineapple
Señorita	Miss

Spanish Pronunciation

- V

In Spanish v at the beginning of a word is pronounced like b in big.

Practise saying this b sound with these Spanish words.

vino	wine
verano	summer
verde	green
vaso	glass
vale	okay

Spanish Pronunciation

■ Z

In Spanish z is pronounced like the th in thanks.

Practise saying this th sound with these Spanish words.

zumo	juice
zapato	shoe
zona	area
plaza	square
taza	cup

Spanish Pronunciation

Summary

ce, ci and z is th in thanks

e at the end of a word is a – the sound of the first letter of the English alphabet.

ge, gi and j is ch in loch

h is silent

ll is y in yes

ñ is ny in canyon

v at the start of a word is b in big

Spanish Pronunciation

Word Stress

Spanish words are normally stressed on the last syllable.

actor normal papel popular

But if a Spanish word ends in a, e, i, o, u, s or n the stress is on the last-but-one syllable.

nota arte plato intenso

If a Spanish word has an accent (') the stress is on the accent.

bebé melón adiós teléfono

SPAIN GUIDE

The Highlights of Spain

Maps of Mainland Spain and the Spanish Islands

Spain

Spain is a fantastic country. Millions of people visit every year to enjoy the excellent climate, superb beaches, great facilities and the relaxed way of life.

Spain also has wonderful towns and cities, beautiful scenery and some of the most enjoyable festivals anywhere in Europe.

In the next few pages we have described the different regions of Spain and highlighted our favourite places to visit. We have also recommended the best food and drink available in each region.

Southern Spain

Andalucía covers all of southern Spain and runs for over 350 miles from the Portuguese border in the west to the province of Almería in the east. Andalucía is a beautiful and popular region of Spain.

There are excellent beaches all along the coastline. The best beaches are on the Atlantic coast of the Costa de la Luz and along the Mediterranean coast of Almería. Inland there are dramatic mountain ranges and beautiful landscapes.

The cities of Granada, Córdoba and Seville have some of the most interesting and important monuments in Europe and are great places to visit. Andalucía is also famous for some of the most colourful and exciting festivals held in Spain.

Highlights of Southern Spain

Places to Visit

Granada's Alhambra palace and gardens. Córdoba's Mezquita mosque and the old town. Seville's Alcázar palace and gardens, Giralda tower and old town. The attractive towns and cities of Cádiz, Jerez and Ronda.

Food and Drink

chilled soups	gazpacho & salmorejo
fried fish	fritura de pescado
cured ham	jamón ibérico
bar snacks	tapas

draught beer	caña
dry sherry	fino & manzanilla
fruit punch	sangría
red wine & lemonade	tinto de verano

Eastern Spain

Eastern Spain consists of the regions of Cataluña, Valencia and Murcia. This large region stretches for over 500 miles from the French border in the north to Andalucía in the south.

This region has some of the best scenery in Spain. The Costa Brava, the area around Dénia and the Mar Menor are exceptionally beautiful. The east coast is home to some of the best known holiday resorts in Spain attracting millions of visitors because of the excellent climate, great beaches and superb facilities.

Barcelona is the cultural and commercial capital of Cataluña and one of the best cities in Europe. Valencia and Murcia are also important and attractive regional capitals.

Highlights of Eastern Spain

Places to Visit

Barcelona's Sagrada Familia cathedral, Gaudi's buildings and Park Güell, the old town and La Rambla. Valencia's historic centre and City of Arts and Sciences. Alicante's beach, seafront and marina. The attractive centres of Gerona, Murcia, Elche and Cartagena.

Food and Drink

paella & rice dishes	arroces
shellfish & noodles	fideuá
Catalan sausage	butifarra
fresh salad	ensalada
fresh fruit	fruta del tiempo
sparkling wine	cava
white wines	Penedés region
red wines	Priorato region
rosé wines	Ampurdán

Northern Spain

Northern Spain includes the regions of Galicia, Asturias, Cantabria, the Basque Country and Navarra. It runs for 350 miles from the Atlantic in the west to the Pyrenees in the east. This area has a cooler and wetter climate than the rest of the country and is sometimes called "Green Spain".

The coastline of Galicia is especially beautiful and there are excellent beaches all along the north coast. The mountains of the Picos de Europa and the Spanish Pyrenees have some of the best scenery in Spain.

This region hosts the beautiful resorts of San Sebastián and Santander and the attractive cities of Santiago de Compostela, Oviedo and La Coruña. Bilbao is home to the fantastic Guggenheim Museum.

Highlights of Northern Spain

Places to Visit

Santiago de Compostela's **cathedral
and old town.** San Sebastián's **bay,
beaches and headlands.** Santander's
bays and beaches. Oviedo's **old town.**

The stunning coastline of Galicia.

Food and Drink

fresh fish	pescados
seafood	mariscos
tuna pie	empanada de atún
bean stew	fabada asturiana
blue cheese	cabrales
white wines	Albariño, Ribeiro, Rías Baixas
cider	sidra
liqueur	orujo

Central Spain

Central Spain covers a huge area from Andalucía in the south to Asturias and Cantabria in the north, from the Portuguese border in the west to Cataluña, Valencia and Murcia in the east. To the south of Madrid there is Castille La Mancha and Extremadura and to the north Castille and León, La Rioja and Aragón.

This massive plain has incredible blue skies throughout the year and is only broken up by mountain ranges to the north and west of Madrid.

Spain's fantastic capital city is in the centre of this region and almost exactly in the centre of Spain. Around Madrid cities like Salamanca, Segovia, Toledo and Ávila are some of the most historic and beautiful cities in Spain.

Highlights of Central Spain

Places to Visit

Madrid's **Plaza Mayor, Royal Palace and
the Thyssen, Prado and Reina Sofía
museums. The Retiro Park and gardens.**
León's **cathedral and old town.**
Salamanca's **Plaza Mayor and old town.**
Ávila's **city walls and historic centre.**
Segovia's **Alcázar and aqueduct.**
Toledo's **cathedral, historic centre and
El Greco paintings.**

Food and Drink

roast lamb	cordero asado
suckling pig	cochinillo asado
ratatouille	pisto manchego
ham	jamón ibérico
cheese	queso manchego
red wines	Rioja, Ribera del Duero
white wines	Rueda, Rioja

The Spanish Islands

Spain has two groups of islands, the Balearic Islands in the Mediterranean and the Canary Islands off the coast of Morocco in the Atlantic.

The Balearic Islands consist of Mallorca, Menorca, Ibiza and Formentera. The Balearics have stunning coastlines, beautiful coves, excellent beaches and some of the best tourist facilities in Europe. Palma de Mallorca, Ibiza and Mahón are lively and attractive capital cities.

The Canary Islands are Gran Canaria, Lanzarote, Fuerteventura, Tenerife, La Gomera, El Hierro and La Palma. The Canaries have an excellent year round climate, dramatic volcanic landscapes, some excellent beaches and vibrant capital cities in Las Palmas de Gran Canaria and Santa Cruz de Tenerife.

Highlights of the Islands

Places to Visit

Balearics - Palma, Ibiza, Mahón and
Ciutadella. The beaches of northern
Mallorca, southern Menorca and Ibiza.
Canaries - Las Palmas, Santa Cruz de
Tenerife. The beaches of Gran Canaria
and Fuerteventura. Volcanic landscapes
in Lanzarote and Tenerife.

Food and Drink

Balearics

breakfast pastry	ensaimada
Menorcan cheese	queso de Mahón
local wine	Binissalem

The Canaries

fresh fish	pescados
salted potatoes	papas arrugadas
spicy sauce	mojo colorado
rum	ron

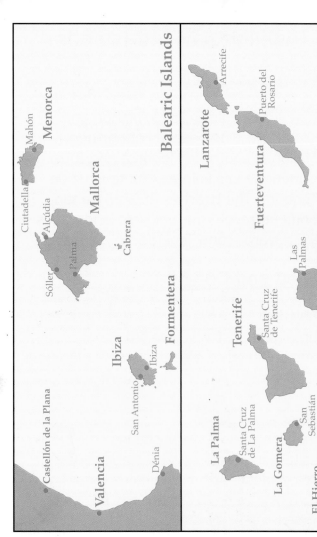

Balearic Islands

Menorca
Mahón
Ciutadella

Mallorca
Alcúdia
Sóller
Palma
Cabrera

Ibiza
San Antonio
Ibiza
Formentera

Castellón de la Plana

Valencia
Dénia

Lanzarote
Arrecife

Fuerteventura
Puerto del Rosario

Gran Canaria
Las Palmas

Canary Islands

Tenerife
Santa Cruz de Tenerife

La Palma
Santa Cruz de la Palma

La Gomera
San Sebastián

El Hierro
Valverde